GW01312051

Kuji Goshin Hou

Sacred Sounds and Gestures

九字護身法

Kuji Goshin Hou

Sacred Sounds and Gestures

Dr. James Clum

Introduction

Thank you for selecting this book on Kuji Goshin Hou. This book is a direct and accurate translation of a small book I purchased which originally came from Japan that was written entirely in Japanese Kanji, Hiragana and Siddham script. Siddham script is an ancient language of Indian origins that was originally used to write down the correct pronunciation of *mantra* (sacred syllables) that were used with *mudra* (sacred hand seals) like the ones in this book. A short translation into English came with the book and was written by a Mr. A. Yamasaki. His translation was good but very brief. I desired to look into each and every word myself to get a richer and more detailed understanding. The only way to do this was to sit down and do the research necessary to come up with a more detailed and comprehensive translation. As you will see, visualization is extremely important in the practice of Shingon or Tendai Buddhism which use these hand seals and sacred syllables. To the extent that one can better visualize what one is concentrating on, the more deep the focus and fruits of these practices. This will go beyond just the translation of this original text and hopefully explain how to use it on a practical level that will transcend language, culture, and belief systems.

Japan is a country that has spent many a century engaged in civil war and feudal disputes. Warfare was elevated to the level of a supreme art form as a result of these times. By trial and error, every aspect of warfare became more and more refined over time. In modern times, the government spends massive amounts of money to insure that soldiers in the American military have the latest technology available to improve the chances of success and survival in the field. In this sense things were no different once in Japan. In Japan however, skills and equipment, although important, were not the sole factors determining military success. The Japanese soldier of the past sought to petition the help of gods from the metaphysical world to assist them in battle. This would essentially give them the spiritual edge that their enemies may not have had. This book contains the instructions and methods used to call upon the spirit world as warriors of Japan had once done to form an unstoppable fortress in one's favor. This is really the essence of using the Kuji Goshin Hou for warriors.

The mudra or "hand seals" came to Japan in the 8th Century by way of Kukai (aka Kobo Daishi). Kukai lived from 774-835 and is probably one of the most significant figures in Japanese history. He is the founder of a sect of Buddhism called Shingon, and also created the phonetic alphabet of Japanese. Kukai traveled to China and received the full transmission of the Esoteric Buddhist teachings that were taught by his teacher Hui Guo. Kukai had a remarkable ability to learn language and was able to navigate through not only Chinese texts but Sanskrit as well. The use of *mandalas, mudra, mantra* and ritual objects like *vajra* are characteristically seen in Shingon. Kukai put an emphasis on *sanmitsu* meaning the "three secrets." This refers to the importance of thoughts, words and actions as being essential to the focus of the mind. One must keep in mind that the original and proper use of *mudra* and *mantra* is for spiritual refinement and not for personal protection.

In the practice of Kuji Goshin Hou, our thoughts focus on the deities being summoned. Our words on one level have meaning, but in some cases the meaning has been lost over time. More importantly the words are sounds which should be voiced in such a way that they make vibrations in the head. These vibrations in turn have an affect on focusing the mind, and connecting to the spirit world. The hand seals or *mudra* as they are often called, are a way of intertwining the fingers in such a way that they create shapes that have symbolic significance within Buddhism. At the same time, they are said to affect energy circuits within the body. Therefore, the goal of meditation in Shingon is not to clear the mind of all thoughts. Rather, the purpose is to focus the mind and arrive at a transcendental state by using thoughts, words, and actions.

Mudra in general and specifically Kuji Goshin Hou have often been portrayed as secret practices exclusive to ninja. This has been perpetuated by books, magazines, movies and anime. In reality, the Kuji Goshin Hou would have been practiced not only by some ninja, but by samurai and especially monks. Tall tales have been spun about ninja who used *kuji in* (hand seals) to disappear or temporarily bind their adversary in an immoveable state. More than the actual effectiveness of the techniques, this speaks mostly to the power of suggestion and the superstitious beliefs of the times.

The use of the Kuji Goshin Hou should be orally transmitted from teacher to student. By this I mean from priest to disciple ideally. Certain essential elements are not in this book, and they must only be taught by oral transmission. I approach this book not as a student or disciple but rather academically as a researcher. I am presenting to you an actual outline of how these methods have been done, and caution the reader to do the same. Regardless of your reason for reading this, I would ask the reader to keep an open mind, and use these methods with righteous intentions.

I would hope that one could apply the principles in this book to one's own meditation practice in a useful and tangible way. Even for the average Japanese person, the Shinto and Buddhist deities mentioned in this book may be unfamiliar. For the western reader, these deities are completely foreign and therefore risk being irrelevant. If one is interested in performing the Kuji Goshin Hou exactly as it is presented here, then I would suggest learning more about Buddhism first as a foundation. If one does not believe and understand the context of these thoughts, words and deeds then it is unlikely that one can derive any meaningful practice from these seals. If one realizes that the whole structure of the Kuji Goshin Hou is to focus the mind and to summon help to meet the challenges of life, then one can apply this to one's own belief system.

Dr. James Clum

Transmission of the Nine Secret Prayers

九字密修法伝

抑も大摩利支天九字の秘法は古来非常の霊験ある一大神法として尊重さらるものである若し夫之を習熟して一旦其堂奥に入らは,獨精神統一若くば心魂安泰の妙境に至り得るばかりでなく.水難火難病難等諸難を免れ得るのである.其他山野,戦地又は夜中一人旅行等總じて我身に重大なる災害のあらんとする時にも之を行ずべし.何事も避くる事神伝妙術なり.

法は毎朝早く其越ちて流ひ口漱ぎ北へ向ひ濁気を吐捨て.東方に向つて口を開き息を吸込こと三度次で歯を叩く三十六度.気を下して心を安静にし左に記す秘文を唱是を修すべし.御降臨を乞ふ秘文.

謹而奉勸御祉無き此所に降臨鎮座給して神祇の祓可壽可壽平けく安らけく聞し食して願ふ所を感應納受なさしめ給へ誠恐誠惶降烈来座 敬白.
大哉賢哉乾元享利貞如律令

(translation of next page)

Nine Secret Prayers Transmission

The secret methods of the Great War God Marishiten have been regarded as miraculous and extraordinary divine methods since ancient times.   Once a person becomes skilled by entering into the secret knowledge, he obtains as well the focus of a concentrated mind that will be like the most serene and beautiful place. One is rescued from calamities of fire and water, illnesses and so on... as well as many other catastrophes. When in battle in the mountains or fields or traveling alone in the middle of the night, perform these prayers to avoid grave personal misfortune. By this marvelous art of divine transmission one can avoid whatever misfortune awaits.

Get oneself up early every morning, rinse the mouth, face the north, and breathe out. Face the east, open the mouth, inhale three times and clack the teeth thirty-six times. Bring the breath down, and rest the mind as you recall the secret formula and chant it so that you master it well.

An Honorable Request While Looking at the Secret Formulas…

I humbly offer this advice to all in attendance in this place so that you won't grant favors or receive compensation for bestowing longevity and exorcising spirits. As you listen and take this in, I hope all here feel the obligation to accept this promise with sincerity.

Sincerely,
 Hiroya Masaya, Kengen Era

 Adhere firmly to the principles of the Buddhas and legal codes.

Visualizing the Deities

Using these seals and sacred syllables one calls upon the spirits and deities of the spirit realms. Why call upon a god you know nothing about? That does not make much sense does it? The goal of this section is to clarify what actually each deity looks like and represents. As you read each description try to visualize each with as much visual clarity as you can until you can animate the figures in your mind. In some cases these descriptions will be filled with symbolism unique to Buddhism, I will try to clarify the meaning in such cases. However, it is not essential that one continue or even start with visualizing these descriptions. In the case of the second example *Bishamonten* (God of Warriors), the figure is dressed in armor as it would have been many centuries ago and carries a bladed pole weapon. That does not mean that this deity is somehow forever entrenched in antiquity. This deity is in essence a creation of the mind beyond the parameters of time and space. So, as you visualize this figure, you may also begin to visualize your own *Bishamonten*. What would he look like dressed in modern armor? What battles are you fighting? What imaginary figure of your own creation would defend you? What would he or she wear? What would he or she carry as weapons? What would he or she do to shield you and from what? As you read about each deity refer back to the first nine hand seals and the deities that are mentioned. I will cover them now in the order they were presented.

金剛合掌
(Kongou Gasshou)

The Joined Palms of the Diamond Realm

手を合せ指先をまじへる
The hands are together with the fingertips not crossed

南無本尊會界摩利支天来臨影向其甲守護令給
namu honzon rukai marishiten rairin ekou sono ko shu go shimetamae

Hail Buddhas of the realms- join together and Marishiten approach to armor, protect, defend and command.

Chant this

たんあぢちゃやまりしやそわか
Ten A Ji Cha Ya Ma Ri Shi Ya So Wa Ka

Below-The Hands in Gassho

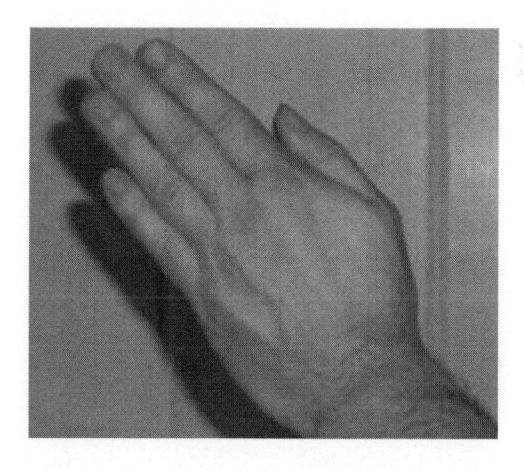

切り紙九字の大事
The Importance of Cutting
the Kuji

九字の切方は圖解を以て左に記しあれば此圖面の
通り行ふ時は自ら覚めなり
Remember the kuji diagrams and perform them
while doing prayer for awakening.

臨

Rin (To Summon)

耶昧三賢普
Fu Gen Sanmaya
(Samantabhadra Bodhisattva) or Vow of Universal
Compassion)

天照皇太神宮毘沙門天
Ten Shou Kou Tai Gen Gu Bi Sha Mon Ten

God of the Illuminated Sky Vaisravana (Guardian God of
Buddhism) and Bishamonten

(The God of Warriors)

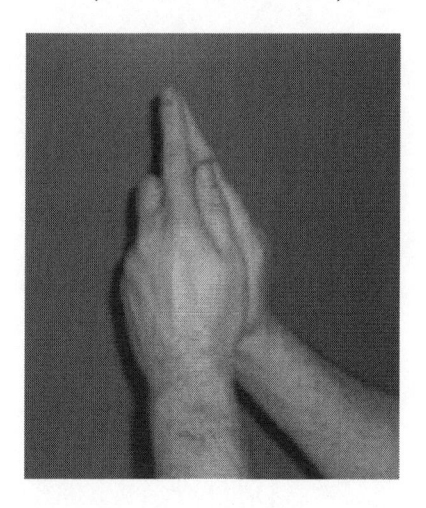

左右二手内縛して二頭指を堅し合して圖の如して,臨と
唱ふべん
You should put the left and right hands together in an
inner bond so the index fingers are vertical like the
picture and then say "Rin.

Bishamonten
(The God of War)

Tenshou Koutai Gengu (Vaisravana the Guardian of the North)

Vaisravana is also called the Deva-raja Vaisravana or Guardian King of the North. He is a diety that was granted great wealth and the ability to grant wealth to others. His generosity is only for those who will further charitable causes or the *Dharma* (Buddhist Way or Law) and those who seek his help and receive it must be charitable to others or they will do harm to themselves. Although pictured in many different ways he is a male figure holding a parasol in his right hand and a mongoose in the left hand. Sometimes he rides a lion. The mongoose is often seen spitting out jewels. The parasol represents his authority over the north and the mongoose which kills snakes represents generosity and good fortune triumphing over greed and hatred as represented by the snake.

How would you personify generosity?

Bishamonten (The God of Warriors)

Bishamonten is another name for Vaisravana. Bishamonten is the God of War and the God of Warriors. His job is to watch over armies that protect the Dharma. He is represented as a soldier in armor holding a long bladed weapon in his left hand and a pagoda in his right hand. He is one of the four directional gods and is the leader among them. He represents victory in conflicts such as war but also victory against ignorance, disease and poverty. He grants favors of good fortune, good health and victory. The weapon is symbolic of his defense of the *Dharma* from evil, and the pagoda contains rewards both material and spiritual which he distributes generously to all who ask for his help and are deserving.

How would you personify triumph over ignorance, disease and poverty?

兵

Byou (Soldier, Army)

輪剛金大
Dai Kon Go Rin
(The Great Diamond Wheel)

正八幡大神十一面觀世音
Shou Hachi Man Jin Ju Ichi Kan Ze On

(The Great Spirit of the Eight Banner War God

The Eleven Faced Goddess of Mercy)

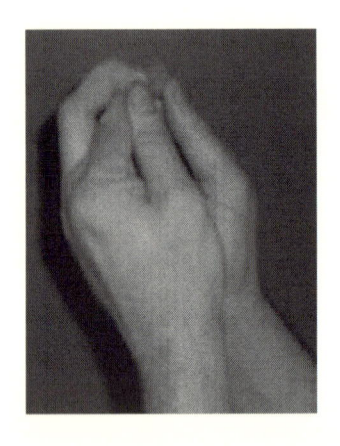

手内縛して二頭指を堅し二中指を舒べ二頭指の背を越へ
て纏ひ合せ二大指を二頭指の間 に堅て合し,兵と唱ふ

Both hands are in an inner bond, the two index fingers
stick up, the two middle fingers stretch around the back
of the two index fingers, the thumbs and index fingers
join and say "Byou."

Juichimen Kannon
(The Eleven Headed Avalokitesvara)

Shou Hachiman (The Eight Banner War God)

Hachiman means "Eight Banners" and is the name given to the 15th Emperor Ojin. As the story goes, banners fell from the heavens to Ojin and thus he got his name. There are thousands of Hachiman shrines in Japan. The attributes of this particular deity have changed over time. It is believed that the emperor Ojin became a god in the Shinto tradition. However, Hachiman is considered a *bodhisattva* in Buddhism as well. He is like a patron saint of warriors and archers if one may describe him as such. Hachiman is typically pictured as a Buddhist monk holding a scepter and sitting on top of a lotus. He is essentially a protector or guardian deity.

Describe the qualities that your own personal guardian must have?

Juichi Kanzeon (Avalokitesvara or the Eleven Headed Goddess of Compassion and Mercy)

There are 33 different manifestations of this *bodhisattva*. A *bodhisattva* is a person who has attained a level of enlightenment but will not pass into Nirvana (paradise) until all sentient beings have passed before them. Avalokitesvara is represented both as a female and male figure that is widely worshipped and sometimes called Kannon which means something like "the one who listens to everyone." The deity wears a crown with faces pointing in every direction and this symbolizes that the deity listens to the prayers of everyone everywhere in the past, present and future.

How do you personify compassion?

鬪

Tou (v. To Fight or Quarrel)

子獅外
Ge Ji Shi
The Outer Lion

春日大明神如意輪觀世音
Kasu Ga Daimyo Jin Nyoi Rin Kanzemon
Great Spirit of Kasuga and Cintamani-cakra (Wish
Fulfilling Avalokitesvara)

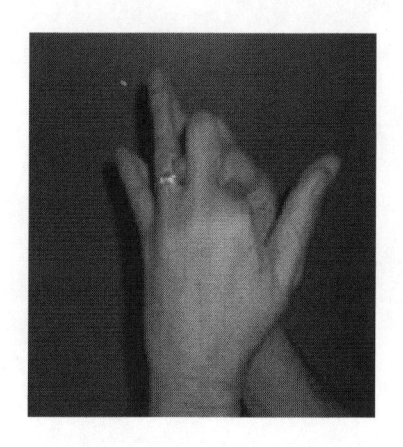

右の頭指の尖を左の中指と無名指との間に入れ左の頭指
も同じく右の中指との間に入れ,左右の中指を以て頭指
を纏ひ大指無名指小指を堅し合す,小指と無名指との間
を少し開き鬪と唱ふ(圖は側面より見たる形)

Insert the tip of the right index finger over the left index
finger yet in between the left middle finger and the ring
finger. Similarly, do the same thing on the other side with
the left index finger. The touching thumbs, ring fingers
and little fingers stand up straight. Say "Tou."

Nyoirin Kannon
(The Wish Fulfilling Goddess of Mercy)

Kasuga Daimyojin (The Great Deities of Kasuga)

In Japan, Kasuga is the site of Shinto/Buddhist shrine and temple complex associated with the Fujiwara family and its guardian deities. It is believed by some that the area itself is holy ground or Pure Land on Earth. Pure Land here I will simply define as a realm of complete enlightenment. The term could be considered controversial depending on how it is defined by individual Buddhist sects.

What are places of personal significance to you that you would deem too personal for others?
Imagine what a guardian of these places would be like.

Jin Nyoi Rin Kanzemon (The Wish Fulfilling Guardian of Compassion and Mercy)

This is another manifestation of Avalokitesvara or the Goddess of Mercy as sometimes she is referred to. In this manifestation the deity is presented as a six-armed *bodhisattva* holding a jewel and a wheel. The jewel could represent the preciousness of the Buddha's teaching. Sometimes the term "three jewels" is used referred in Buddhism to mean the Buddha, his teachings, and the followers. The wheel represents the dharma or Buddhist Law. Simply put it is the teaching of the Buddha. This deity has many of the same attributes as other manifestations of Avalokitesvara. This deity however fulfills one's wishes if the wish is consistent with the *Dharma*.

How would you personify a facilitator of your own dreams?

者

Sha (Person, People)

子獅内
Nai Ji Shi
The Inner Lion

加茂大明神不動明王
Kamo Daimyoujin Fudou Myouou
The Great Spirit of Kamo and the Immoveable
Manifestation of Mahavairocana

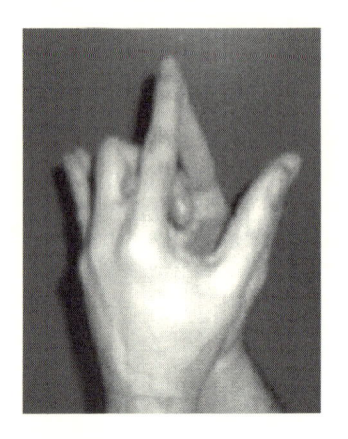

右の無名指の尖を左の中指と頭指との間に入れ左の頭指
の尖も同く右の中指との間に入れ,左右の中指を以て無
名指を纏ひ,大指頭指小指を竪し合す,者と唱ふ(圖は側面
より見たる形)

The point of the right ring finger is put between the
middle and index fingers. Similarly the left ring finger
does the same thing. The middle fingers fold over the
the ring fingers. The thumb, index fingers and little
fingers are held vertical. Say "Sha."

Fudo Myou-Ou
(The Immoveable)

Kamo Daimyoujin (The Great Diety of Kamo)

Kamo Daimyojin is a *kami* or "god" in Shintoism. Legend has it that Kamo Daimyoujin was a *kami* that appeared as a monk.

If guardian angels exist/ed what do/would yours look like?

Fudo Myou (The Immoveable One)

Fudo Myou means the Immoveable One. He sits sternly in the lotus position holding a sword in one hand and a rope in the other. He is typically represented with flames surrounding him. Fudo Myou originally was a demon who was converted once he heard Buddha's words. He then became one of the guardians of Buddhism. The sword he holds in his right hand is no ordinary sword. The handle forms a *vajra* which means "diamond" and represents the shattering of all falsehood with truth. This is also the meaning of the sword. It could be seen also as not only the sword that cuts through falsehood exposing truth, but also as a guardian's weapon. Fudo Myou is considered a wrathful deity. The rope in the left hand is a symbol that represents how after one hears the truth one is bound by it. The truth is what makes this deity steadfast. He is not considered a buddha or a bodhisattva but he is widely worshipped especially in Esoteric Buddhism.

Describe what it means in your view to be "a better person?"

皆

Kai (All, Everybody)
縛外

Ge Baku
The Outer Bond

稲荷大明神愛染妙王
Inari Daimyoujin Aizen Myouou
The Great Spirit of Inari (God of Harvests) and Ragaraja
(Buddhist Deity of Love)

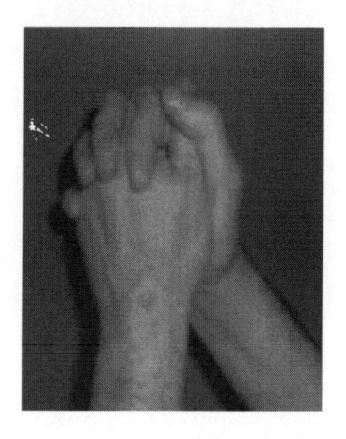

二手各深く指を出して組み合はて,皆と唱ふ
Join the two hands together so all the fingers and firmly
together and say "Kai."

Aizen Myōō
(Deity of Lust Suppression)

Inari Daimyoujin (God of Harvests)

Inari Daimyoujin is worshipped as the God of Harvests. This deity sits upon a calf holding a *vajra* sword in the right hand. Inari is a *yaksha* or benevolent spirit of the land. Sometimes Inari may be represented as a farmer carrying rice. Inari shrines are of Shinto origin and can be found throughout Japan. They characteristically have red *tori* meaning the Shinto gates, and statues of foxes. The fox was a messenger for Inari according to legend, and that is why the two are associated with each other. People in rural areas prayed to Inari Daimyoujin for protection and good harvests.

What does being an advocate of the less fortunate mean to you?

Aizen Myou (The God of Love)

Aizen Myou was a demon who was converted by the truth of Buddhism. Originally he was consumed with anger, hatred, greed and lust, but turned all of these destructive passions into the desire for enlightenment and the advancement of the Buddhist Dharma. He is often pictured seated with six arms in fists. One of his arms holds a *vajra* in front of his chest. He wears a helmet made of a demonic skull and has a third eye. Aizen Myou has a frightful look to him typical of a demon guardian.

Can you think of addictions, habits or obsessions that consume valuable time in your life, and prevent you from getting on with more important things?

陳

Jin (v. to arrange, to state)

内縛
Nai Haku
The Inner Bond

住吉大明神正觀世音
Sumiyoshi Daimyoujin Shou Kanzenon
The Great Spirits of Sumiyoshi(Gods of the Sea) and
Aryavalokitesvara (manifestation of Goddess of
Compassion)

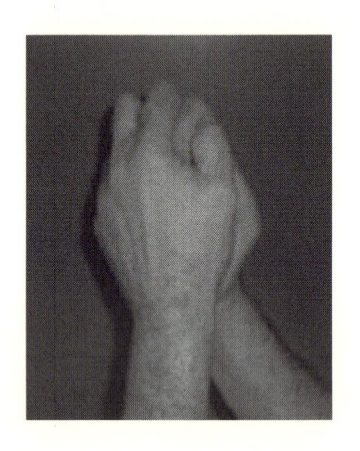

左右十指互に内へ組み入れ,陳と唱ふ

Insert the ten fingers of the left and right hands into one
another and say, "Jin."

Sho Kannon
(Bodhisattva of Mercy and Compassion)

Sumiyoshi Daimyoujin (God of the Sea)

This is another Shinto god commonly worshipped by people who travel by sea. It is located in Sumiyoshi.

Perhaps you can remember being carried in your parents' arms as a child.
Didn't it feel secure and safe?
Do you ever get that feeling now as an adult?

Shou Kanzenon (Goddess of Compassion)

Shou Kanzenon is also called Aryavalokitesvara which is another root manifestation of Avalokitesvara.

Please reflect on individuals who have shown compassion and empathy towards you.

裂

Retsu (to split, to fizzure)

券智
Chi Ken
The Wisdom Bond

丹生大明神阿弥陀如来
Nifu Daimyoujin Amida Nyorai
The Great Spirit of Nifu (God of the Mountains) and the
Amitabha Buddha

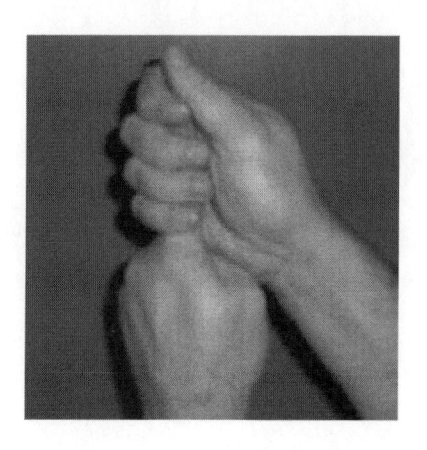

左四指を握りて頭指を竪,右の三指にて左の頭指を握り,
右の大指と頭指と左の頭指との三指の爪尖を合はし,裂
と唱ふ
The left four fingers make a grip while the index finger is
vertical, three fingers of the right hand grip the left index
finger, the right thumb and index finger meet at the
fingertips and say "Retsu."

Amida Nyorai
(The Buddha of Illumination)

Nifu Daimyoujin (God of the Mountains)

This is another Shinto god associated with safe travel through the mountains. Traveling through mountains was not as easy as it is today. In the past centuries ago travel was difficult with only trails instead of roads. Mountains became a sanctuary for bandits and were said to be the home of *tengu* or"human-crows"that would play tricks to scare people.

Please reflect on individuals that have helped you to gain safe passage on your life journeys.

Amida Nyorai (The Buddha of Infinite Light)

The Buddha of Infinite Light is a buddha associated with the Pure Land. In simple terms he is like a savior that guides one to paradise and out of the world of endless death and suffering as a kind of savior figure. Amida Nyourai at one time was named Houzou Bosatsu which meant that he was a bodhisattva. He made 48 vows and after fulfilling all of them became a buddha. One of his vows was to create a paradise or Pure Land in which by chanting *Namu Amida Butsu* (Hail Amida Buddha) sincerely one would go into paradise upon one's death. Amida Nyorai is typically seen sitting in a full lotus position radiating an aura of light. His eyes are closed and he is in a state of deep meditation.

What are the characteristics of a savior to you?

Zai (Located At)

輪日
Nichi Rin
The Sun

日天子弥勒菩薩
Nichi Ten Shi Miroku Bosatsu
The Sun God and the Bodhisattva Maitreya

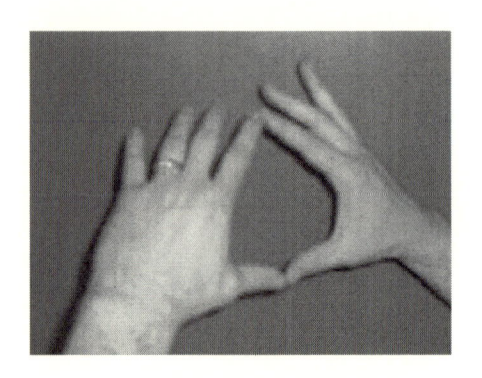

左右の大指と頭指との端を合せ輪日の如く圓くし,餘の
六指を開き散ば之れ後光なり,

在と唱ふ

The edges of the tips of the thumbs and index fingers
join as if to form a circle like the sun, the other six fingers
are open representing a halo. Say "Zai."

Miroku Bosatsu or Maitreya
The Buddha of the Future)

Nichi Tenshi (The Sun God)

This is another Shinto god.

What qualities to we admire in others that could be used to describe the sun?

Miroku Bosatsu (The Buddha of the Future)

Miroku Bosatsu is also commonly called Maitreya. One day he is believed to save Buddhism from extinction. He is often pictured waiting for the prophesy about him to be fulfilled. Therefore, he sits on a thrown with his legs crossed contemplating when his time will come.

Can you think of any historical figure or people who have passed that waited patiently until it was their time to shine?

前

Zen (Front, Before)

形隠

On Gyo
Invisibility

摩利支天文殊菩薩
Marishiten Monju Bosatsu
The God of War and Manjusri the Bodhisattva of
Illumination

左の手をうつろに握り右手にて其上を覆ひ中に容れしも
のを隠す如くし前と唱ふ

Grip the left hand and put it inside the right hand as if to
conceal it,

and then say "Zen."

Marishiten
(The God of Warriors)

Monju Bosatsu
Bodhisattva of Wisdom

Marishiten (The Goddess of the Sun and Moon)

The image of Marishiten is obscured by the blinding light of the sun behind her. At one point in Japanese history she became a patron saint to warriors. Therefore, Marishiten may appear to be riding a wild boar. In this representation, the deity appears as a mad demon holding a sword, a bow and a spear.

In what ways are you fearless?
In what ways are you fearful?

Monju Bosatsu (The Guardian of the Law)

This deity is commonly referred to as Manjusri. He is one of the most common bodhisattvas referred to in Buddhism. He is often pictured sitting in a lotus position with a flaming sword in his right hand and a flower in his left. The sword again represents cutting through ignorance with the truth of the *dharma*. The flower represents the attainment of enlightenment. There are 14 different manifestations of Manjusri. One such manifestation is Yama the God of Death.

What have you learned about yourself through this process of visualization and reflection?

Kuji Kiri

Hold the right fingers as shown in the photo below. Draw the fingers like a sword and proceed to cut this grid in front of you calling out each of the nine Kuji as you make each line. With a final stroke thrust forward into the grid with your hand sword sealing your intention.
(author's explanation)

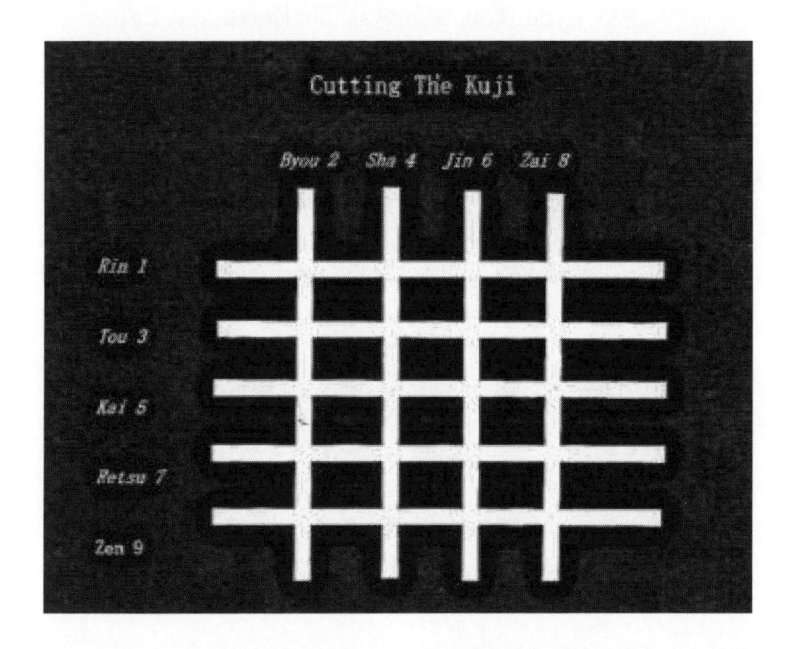

Cutting The Kuji

Byou 2   Sha 4   Jin 6   Zai 8

Rin 1
Tou 3
Kai 5
Retsu 7
Zen 9

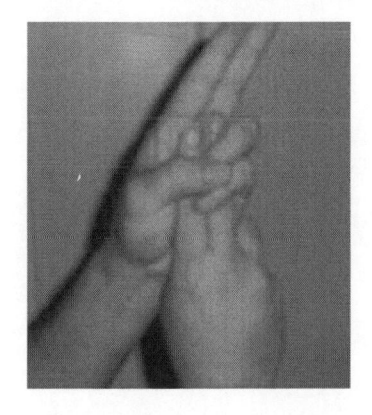 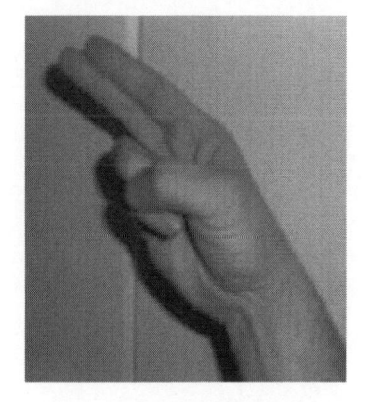

右は即ち指を以て結ぶ大切なる印契であって,其稱呼は
即ち臨兵闘者皆陳裂在前の須序なり

On the right(previous pages) there are fingers used to tie
and to cut the following seals that are called

Rin, Byou, Tou, Sha, Kai, Jin, Retsu, Zai, Zen.

誠心誠意を以て諸印を結び,然る後之を切る,併し之を切
るには刀印以てせよ

Tie the mudra with complete sincerity and afterwards
make a final cut with the sword seal.

九字を戻す法
The Method of Restoring the Kuji
(Meaning to Send the Gods Back to Where They Came From)

On Kiri Kiyara. Hara Hara. Futaran. Posotsu. Sowaka

三遍唱ふべし
You Should Say This Three Times

又送納秘文
The Secret Formula Sending Back

掛け巻も賢き天地神祇爰に降臨一切の諸神等元の本宮へ
御送奉る,恐れなから承引し給へ送納帰宮住社敬白天福
圓満神道神力一切諸諸成就守らせ給へと恐れみ 恐れみ
申白

I offer this sincerely as the gods of heaven and earth
have descended-without exception ....multitudes of
gods...before the main shrine I humbly ask that we we
may receive your heavenly blessing and protect us from
all kinds of misfortune and bring us good fortune,
disembark and return to the shrines where you reside.

毎朝日天子拝見の大事
The Importance of Gazing Upon
Nitten (The Sun Guardian) Every Morning

毎朝早く起きて手流び口漱ぎ東の方日出に向ひて修すべ
し

Every morning at sunrise, get up, wash the hands, rinse
the mouth and face East.

先三禮し
Bow three times.

合掌唱文
Words to Say With Hands Joined in Prayer

南無帰命頂禮大日天子,天照坐日大御神為度衆生故
普照四天下

Namu Ki Myo Cho Rai Nittenshi Amaterashi Mashimasu
Hino O Mikami Yi Do Shu Jyoku Fu Syo Shiten Ge

Hail, Return to Life, Hands Together at the Head I Pray,
Vairocana Buddha, Nitten the Guardian of the Sun,
Amaterasu the Great Goddess of the Sun,
Save All Sentient Beings and Illuminate All Under
Heaven.

印え縛外

Gebaku no In
The Outer Bond Seal

滅即難七
しちなんそくめつ
Shichi Nan Soku Metsu
Namely the Seven Misfortunes

chant

On A Bi Ra Un Ken

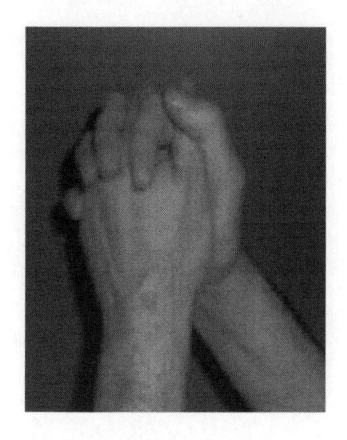

手の指を外へ組合せ
The fingers cross and they are joined on the outside

印え縛内

**Naibaku no In
The Inner Bond Seal**

生即福七
しちなんそくめつ
Shichi Fuku Soku Sho
The Seven Lucky Gods

chant

On Ba Zara Da To Ban

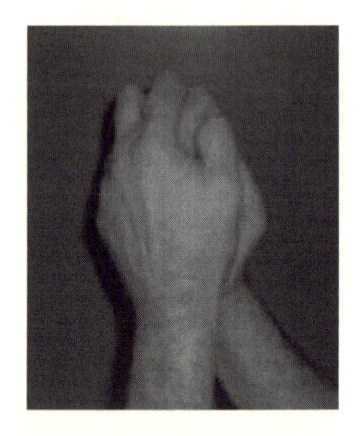

手の指を中へ入れて組む

Cross the finger of the hands inside each other.

日天子御眞言

Nitten Shi Go Shingon

Secret Formula of the Honorable Sun God

Chant

Nomaku Sanmanda Bodanan Anichaya Sowaka

摩利支天 御眞言

Marishiten Go Shingon

Secret Formula of the Honorable War God

Chant

Nomaku Sanmanda Dabodanan Tan Marishi Ei Sowaka

月天子 御眞言

Getten Shi Go Shingon

Secret Formula of the Honorable Moon God

Chant

Nomaku Sanmanda Bodanan Senda Ra Ya Sowaka

不動明王御眞言

Fudo Myouou Go Shingon

**Secret Formula of the Honorable Immoveable
Guardian King**

Chant

Nomaku Sanmanda Bararatan Senda Maka Roshi Ya
Da Sowataya Mudou Da Kanman

合掌

Gasshou

Join the Palms Together

護持某甲哀愍納受

Go Gi Mu Ko Ai Min No Ju

May I have protection, be shielded from grief, and accept compassion.

畢而三禮

Finish with Three Forms of Reverence

Traditionally this meant with right shoulder bare, kneeling, and hands together in prayer.

護身法印明

Go Shin Hou In-Myou

Self-Protection Mudra

淨三業 三部 被甲

Josango, Sanbu, Hikoh

The Three Pure Endeavors, The Three Divisions, The Armor

これを護身法といふ

This is called the Goshin Pou or Self-Protection Methods.

十八印契第一にして,秘密甚深の印言なり

The eighteen mudra become the most deeply secret seals and words.

此法を修せんと欲せば, 身器を清浄にし

If one desires to practice these method, they have the ability to purify the body.

壇上を荘飾して随分に供貝を供へ

Decorate the top of the home altar with plenty offerings.

五体を地に擲ちて本尊を禮したてまつり誠心修行すべし

One should practice this with the entire body on the ground, bowing to Buddha and showing the proper etiquette and sincerity of heart.

如法に行ずれば,身口意につくるところの罪障を消除し

If one performs the teachings of Buddha, using action, speech and thought, sins and other obstacles will be eliminated.

三部諸尊の加護蒙り

Divine protection from suffering through the three groups of Tathagata (Buddhas).

身をして堅固ならしめ, もろもろの魔障魔を降伏し,
水火盗兵一切の厄難の, 恐なからしむ,
誠に難遭遇未會有の密法なれば,謹んで行ひ奉るべし

Humbly ask for a strong body, removal of hinderances to spiritual practice and evil influences, protections from fire and water, soldiers, and complete calamities.

With sincerity encounter not any hardships. Be careful of the Secret Teachings and practice the offerings with utmost respect.

此法は密家に秘重するところなれとも,二三輩の信士の
懇請するに任せて

These methods are to be done secretly in the home, but you may entrust them to a few believers to do on their own.

梓に壽する者なり

You will become a person of longevity.

明印業三浄

Jou San Gyou In-Myou

Purifying the Three Actions

(Body, Words, Actions)

身口意に作る所の諸の罪業をめつして清浄なることを得
せしむる印明也

One's body, speech and actions can become purified
from various types of sins when the Illumination Seal is
used.

Chant

**On So Wa Ban Wa Shu Da Sa Ru Wa Da Ru Ma So
Wa Ban Wa Shu Do Gan**

左右の手を相合し掌中をうつろにすべしこれを虚心合掌
といふ

Both hands join together and you should leave space
between the palms.

This is also called Gasshou.

耶昧三部佛

Butsu Bu San Ma Ya

Buddha Vow

十方三世諸佛の護念を得て壽命をまし福徳を長ず

All buddhas of the past, present and future in all directions protect us from desires, obtain for us long life and let our prosperity grow.

chant

On Ta Ta Gi Ya To To Ban Wa Ya So Wa Ka

前の印にて

Before making the sign.

掌をひらき指の端を二中指の上節につけ二大指屈して頭指の下節に安ず

Space the palms apart, index finger is placed at the top section of the middle finger and the thumbs are bent and placed at the bottom section of the index finger.

耶昧三部華蓮

Ren Ge Bu San Ma Ya

Lotus Vow

觀世音菩薩等の諸のぼさつの加持を得て一切の業障を消
除するなり

Avalokitsvara Bodhisattva, may these many incantations
obtain good karma any remove any obstacles.

chant

On Han Do Ma Do Ban Wa Ya So Wa Ka

左右五指を開き散らして, 大指小指を相つけ, 八
葉蓮華花の形ちの如くなす

The five fingers of both hands are opened creating a
space, the thumbs and little fingers touch so the fingers
become the shape of a lotus flower.

耶昧三部剛金

Kan Gou Bu San Ma Ya

Vajra Vow

金剛部の諸尊の加被を蒙り一さいの病なんをのぞき堅固
の體となる

Deities of the Diamond Realm empower us from all the
ills of ignorance and despair and help us to become
steadfast

chant

On Wa Ji Ro Do Ban Wa Ya So Wa Ka

左掌をかへしふせて外へむけ

Put your left palm to the outside

右をふぎて手の背をつけ,大指小指互ひにはしを引かけ
て鈎の如くなす

The right hand is placed on top and the thumbs and little
finger hook onto each other as though they are pulling
away.

耶昧三部身護

Go Shin Bu San Ma Ya

Self-Protection Vow

諸の天魔の障碍を除,
一切の厄難をよけ身を堅固ならしむ

Save us with empowerment from the obstacles of
demons, and protect us from every evil so that we may
become steadfast.

chant

On Wa Ji Ra Gi Ni Ha Ra Shi Ha Ni Ya So Wa Ka

二手内に交へて

The insides of both hands intersect.

二中指はしを合せて, 二頭指を少しく曲げ,
二大指にて無名指のもとをおす圖の如

Join the middle fingers, the index fingers are a little
curved, and push the thumbs against the index fingers
as in the illustration.

右護身法印契ほ々これを注す，
對譯は儀軌に載するところに從がひ梵音は家の聖にまか
せてにれをしるす，
しかれとも猶 口授に依らざれば佛法の罪その恐ありこ
れを修せんと思は々傳密の先達に就て更に問ふべし

The Goshin Hou In Myou (Self-Protection Seals) that
were presented here were transcribed from a sage of the
Brahmin class; therefore, they are orally instructed and
to practice them otherwise may violate Buddhist law so
be careful as you practice and ask you teacher about
this secret transmission if you want to do it.

不動七傳の印

Fudou Nana Shibari no In

The Seven Transmission Seals of the Immoveable

(不動金縛之秘傳)

Fudou Kana Shibari no Hiden

(The Secret Transmission of the Immoveable Binding)

印縛内
Naibaku In

The Inner Bond Seal

chant

**Nao Ma Ku San Man Da Ba Sa Ra Da Sen Tan Ka Ro
Shi Ya Ta Ya So Ha Ta Ra Ya Un Ta Ra Ta Kan Man**

印劔
Ken In

The Sword Seal

chant

On Ki Ri Ki Ri

印刀
Tou In

The Blade Seal

chant

On Ki Ri Ki Ri

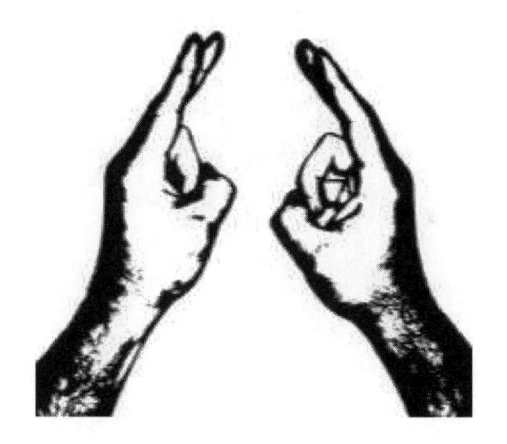

印輪法轉
Ten Hou Rin In

Turning the Wheel of the Law Seal

chant

**No Ma Ku San Man Da Ba Sa Ra Da Sen Da Ma Ka
Ro Shi Ya Ta So Wa Ta Ra Ya Un Ta Ra Ta Kan Man**

印鈷悟外
Ge Go Ko In

The Outer Enlightenment Cobalt Seal

chant

不動大御眞言

Fu Do Dai Go Shin Gon

The Mantra of the Great Immoveable One

勅教天諸
Shoten Kyo Choku

Commanding the Gods

chant

O Ku Ki Ri Un Ki Ya Ku Un

印縛外
Gebaku In

The Outer Bond Seal

chant

**On Ma Ku San Man Da Ba Sa Ra Da Sen Ta Ma Ka Ro
Shi Ta Ya**

So Wa Ta Ra Ya Un Ta Ra Ta Kan Man

Bibliography

Nagato, Soturo. <u>Kuji Goshin Hou</u>. 2nd. Kyoto, Japan: Nagata Funshoudo, 2003.

"Aizen-Myoo." *Encyclopedia Mythica* from Encyclopedia Mythica Online.
<<u>http://www.pantheon.org/articles/a/aizen-myoo.html</u>>
[Accessed July 16, 2009]

Chandra, Dr. Lokesh. "VAISRAVANA/KUVERA IN THE SINO-JAPANESE TRADITION." <u>Burobudor.TV</u>. 2005. 16 Jul 2009 <http://www.borobudur.tv/vaisravana.htm>.

Schumacher, M. (2009). Hachiman & Hachimangū Shrines . Retrieved July 17, 2009, from ." BUDDHISM & SHINTOISM IN JAPAN A TO Z PHOTO DICTIONARY OF JAPANESE SCULPTURE & ART Web site: http://www.onmarkproductions.com/html/tsurugaoka-hachiman.shtml

Schumacher, M. (2008). KANNON BOSATSU, KANNON BODHISATTVA LORD OF COMPASSION, GODDESS OF MERCY . Retrieved July 17, 2009, from ." BUDDHISM & SHINTOISM IN JAPAN A TO Z PHOTO DICTIONARY OF JAPANESE SCULPTURE & ART Web site: http://www.onmarkproductions.com/html/kannon.shtml

Schumacher, M. (2009). Shrines by Type, Shrines by Kami (Deity) . Retrieved July 17, 2009, from ." BUDDHISM & SHINTOISM IN JAPAN A TO Z PHOTO DICTIONARY OF JAPANESE SCULPTURE & ART Web site: http://www.onmarkproductions.com/html/shrine-guide.shtml#kasuga

Schumacher, M. (2009). Buddha and Bodhisattva Directory Avalokitesvara . Retrieved July 17, 2009, from ." BUDDHISM & SHINTOISM IN JAPAN A TO Z PHOTO DICTIONARY OF JAPANESE SCULPTURE & ART Web site: http://www.onmarkproductions.com/html/kannon-popup.shtml

Schumacher, M. (2009). MYŌ-Ō. Retrieved July 17, 2009, from ." BUDDHISM & SHINTOISM IN JAPAN A TO Z PHOTO DICTIONARY OF JAPANESE SCULPTURE & ART Web site: http://www.onmarkproductions.com/html/myo-o.shtml

Schumacher, M. (2009). Aizen Myo-o. Retrieved July 17, 2009, from ." BUDDHISM & SHINTOISM IN JAPAN A TO Z PHOTO DICTIONARY OF JAPANESE SCULPTURE & ART Web site: http://www.onmarkproductions.com/html/myo-o.shtml

Schumacher, M. (2007). Inari. Retrieved July 17, 2009, from ." BUDDHISM & SHINTOISM IN JAPAN A TO Z PHOTO DICTIONARY OF JAPANESE SCULPTURE & ART Web site: http://www.onmarkproductions.com/html/oinari.shtml

Schumacher, M. (2008). Kannon. Retrieved July 17, 2009, from ." BUDDHISM & SHINTOISM IN JAPAN A TO Z PHOTO DICTIONARY OF JAPANESE SCULPTURE & ART Web site: http://www.onmarkproductions.com/html/kannon.shtml# ShoKannon

Schumacher, M. (2009). Amida Buddha. Retrieved July 17, 2009, from ." BUDDHISM & SHINTOISM IN JAPAN A TO Z PHOTO DICTIONARY OF JAPANESE SCULPTURE & ART Web site: http://www.onmarkproductions.com/html/amida.shtml

Schumacher, M. (2009). Miroku Nyorai. Retrieved July 17, 2009, from ." BUDDHISM & SHINTOISM IN JAPAN A TO Z PHOTO DICTIONARY OF JAPANESE SCULPTURE & ART Web site: http://www.onmarkproductions.com/html/miroku.shtml

Schumacher, M. (2009). OTHER TENBU (DEVA). Retrieved July 17, 2009, from ." BUDDHISM & SHINTOISM IN JAPAN A TO Z PHOTO DICTIONARY OF JAPANESE SCULPTURE & ART Web site: http://www.onmarkproductions.com/html/kankiten-idaten-other-tenbu.html>

Schumacher, M. (2009). Monju Bosatsu Guardian of Buddhist Law. Retrieved July 17, 2009, from ." BUDDHISM & SHINTOISM IN JAPAN A TO Z PHOTO DICTIONARY OF JAPANESE SCULPTURE & ART Web site: http://www.onmarkproductions.com/html/monju.shtml

All pen and ink drawings were done by James Clum.

9549811R00042

Printed in Great Britain
by Amazon.co.uk, Ltd.,
Marston Gate.